THE NEW AMERICAN FAMILY
AND THE SCHOOL

by

J. Howard Johnston

NATIONAL MIDDLE SCHOOL ASSOCIATION

nmsa

Dr. J. Howard Johnston is one of the middle school movement's best known and most articulate spokesmen. His words and wisdom have regularly appeared in the *Middle School Journal* and NMSA monographs.

The Association is grateful to Dr. Johnston, a University of Cincinnati professor, for his willingness to share this combination of his scholarship and writing competence in addressing a topic of critical importance.

Copyright © 1990 by the National Middle School Association
4807 Evanswood Drive, Columbus, Ohio 43229
$6.00

The materials presented herein are the expressions of the author and do not necessarily represent the policies of NMSA.

Printed in the United States of America by
Panaprint, Inc., P. O. Box 10297, Macon, Ga 31297

ISBN: 1-56090-047-4

Table of Contents

Dedication

For the family that has taught me so much about love, the celebration of diversity, and the New American Family. To Joanne, Kristin, Alex, Carlos, Fletcher, Carol, George, Marietta, Mom and Dad.

FOREWORD

However reluctantly, Americans are coming to grips with the changing American family. These changes are not just projections of what is to be in the future, they are ones that have already taken place. Whatever the causes -- and there are many -- it is no longer possible to operate our lives effectively on old assumptions about the structure and composition of the family. Nearly every facet of our society is impacted by the alterations that have occurred in the family unit from the kinds of housing being constructed, to the types of food in the supermarkets, to the child care services needed -- even to the approaches used in advertising automobiles. But perhaps no institution is impacted more than is the school.

Since families have changed dramatically, so too should schools. Yet schools have been more resistant to change than any of our institutions. A modern day Rip Van Winkle after a fifty year sleep would find himself lost and out of place in our kitchens, on our highways, in our businesses, nearly everywhere but in our schools. Only in the classroom would he be "at home." Schools have seemed unable or unwilling to alter the nature of their programs or the arrangements under which they are provided. This condition must change.

This monograph will provide an essential tool in the reordering of the home-school connection. Based on an extensive review of the literature, the first chapter provides a dramatic profile of the new American family. A second chapter draws on the works of recognized scholars in discussing the sometimes overlooked educational influences of the family.

The third chapter details the barriers to home-school cooperation that exist. While some may be inevitable, others are caused by old assumptions and insensitivities. A final chapter, "Involving Families in Schooling," is especially important and helpful in pointing out specific steps to take in improving the often fractured relationship between school and home.

Throughout this volume there runs a clear challenge to schools -- educators must acquire an adequate understanding of the changes that have taken place in the family, assess traditional practices, and take the initiative in involving parents in new and functional ways.

The monograph is direct and forthright. It provides a basis for understanding much parental behavior that is often misjudged. It lays bare some realities and puts to rest some old myths. This publication is not just for the middle level, it is equally applicable to elementary and high schools for children in a family are usually enrolled in more than one level and, of course, move rapidly to another level.

Seldom does so much significant information and assistance come in so small a package. *The New American Family and the Schools* is truly a volume of immense importance.

John H. Lounsbury

INTRODUCTION

Out Of The Past

"Ward, I'm worried about the Beaver." With those words, spoken to her husband, June Cleaver led us, enthralled, into one of the "Leave It to Beaver" episodes that were to become the archetype for American family life in the middle of the Twentieth Century. It was a time when the big problems, like World War II, the Nazi Holocaust, Corregidor, Hiroshima and Nagasaki were behind us. And it was a time when the awesome legacy of those events, racism, pollution, nuclear proliferation, and global poverty, were not yet in the American vernacular. We were lucky to be alive and living in the good old USA, and we celebrated our good fortune with the gusto of an adolescent nation still somewhat astonished by its own might.

What could go wrong? Listening to June, Ward, Wally and the Beaver, we would conclude, "not much." The problem that concerned Mrs. Cleaver? Well it was complicated enough to engage us for half an hour but simple enough to be resolved, with the proper moral lesson, in the same time. Memory dims after twenty-five years, but it seems that Beaver agreed to keep a rabbit for a friend who was going on vacation, but had neglected to get his parent's permission. There he was in the garage, hiding the rabbit, when elder brother Wally found him and warned him of his parents' impending wrath ("Boy. Dad is really gonna be mad when he finds out you used his new picnic blanket as a rabbit bed.")

June noticed right away, of course, that the Beaver was concealing some dark secret because he didn't eat his favorite dessert. With gentle prodding, she and Ward extracted the confession and, after reprimanding Beaver (not for helping a friend but for not telling them) helped make the rabbit comfortable for the next two weeks. The moral? Don't ever conceal things from your parents, because your own guilt will keep you from enjoying even your favorite things.

Those episodes, combined with other elements of the popular culture of the day, inexorably shaped our view of families. And even if the one on the screen

1

wasn't like ours, it seemed that it showed the way families were <u>supposed</u> to be. Ward lived with June; the boys went to school every day and their parents made sure their homework was done before they ran off to play baseball; Dad never got drunk or hit the boys; Mom never lost her temper; no one used alcohol or drugs; everyone worked hard and had enough money; and no conflict that arose ever lasted more than thirty minutes.

Most of us do not have to look very far into our own personal histories, though, to find out that the Cleavers lived only on the screen and in our collective imaginations about what we <u>wished</u> all families to be. After the war, we all had money problems. Many lived with chemically dependent parents in unhappy marriages. Others lived with single parents who struggled endlessly against economic dislocation. There were abundant numbers of working poor who had inadequate medical care and housing. Schools were segregated and racial violence was all too clearly in evidence.

There was, however, a powerful, if unspoken agreement among Americans that family problems were to be kept in the family. It was not until the 1960s that "family" problems, such as chemical abuse, poverty and domestic violence became social policy issues, and the hidden problems of unhappy marriages, teenage pregnancy and a host of others came out of the nation's closet and into our mainstream institutions: the courts, the press, and, most important for us, the <u>schools</u>.

CHAPTER ONE

The New American Family In Profile

Beyond the growing public awareness of family issues, it is true that the family has changed dramatically since the 1950s. Two working parents has become the norm rather than the exception in most intact families. In addition, other structures and family arrangements have also emerged that are somewhat less common but no less influential on the lives of our children and the ways in which schooling is conducted in America. Even a cursory review of readily available sources such as the *Information Please Almanac* points to a radically different America.

Household Composition

Between 1950 and 1985 the divorce rate more than doubled while the marriage rate declined somewhat. Just under 50% of all marriages now end in divorce.

As a result of this and other trends, the American household has changed dramatically. There are over 10 million female headed households (about 20% of all US households) with no husband present. Just over 2.4 million single male headed households exist. More importantly for schools, though, virtually all of the children being raised by single parents are being raised by females.

Household size has also shrunken dramatically. Through the 1930s, 1940s and 1950s, the average US household contained approximately four people. It was the "typical family" of a working parent, a home-maker parent and one or more dependent children. Indeed, even in 1960, 60% of all US households were constituted in that way. By 1980, however, only 11% of American households looked like that of 1960; by 1983 the proportion had shrunken to 7%, and by 1988 was estimated to be less than 4%. Now, the average size of a US household is just over two residents. This means that many families are having to cope with a smaller "human resource" in managing necessary affairs, such as generating income, providing child care, or caring for an aging parent.

While part of this trend is due to divorce, another portion is due to the large number of elderly people who are living longer and living alone after the death of a spouse. Some estimates place the number of households comprised of single people over the age of 65 at 8.4 million, or approximately 12% of all households in the US! Of this number, approximately 6.5 million households are single females; 1.7 million are male.

Childbirth

Between the turn of the 20th Century and 1987, the birthrate was halved in the US. A large portion of that decline (nearly 25%) occurred between the mid-1950s and the present. At the same time, however, the birth rates have increased dramatically for certain segments of the population, particularly minorities and immigrants. (Hodgkinson, 1985)

In the 1980's, the birth rates for diverse groups were as follows:

Cubans	1.3 per couple
Whites	1.7
Puerto Ricans	2.1
Blacks	2.4
Mexican-Americans	2.9

A birthrate of 2.1 per couple is required for an ethnic or racial group to stay even, or simply replace itself. Clearly,then, the white and Caribbean Hispanic population is likely to decline while the Black and Mexican-American population will increase rather dramatically.

In fact, the drama of the population increases outlined above will be even more profound when the average age of each ethnic group is considered. The average age of white Americans is 31 years, compared with the average for Blacks of 25 and for Mexican Americans of 22. Thus, the white population, with its low birthrate, is leaving its childbearing years, while the average Hispanic female is just entering them. That is why the state of California has become the first "majority of minorities" state in the US. Its large Hispanic population, with a low average age and high birthrate, creates a population momentum with dramatic effects on the demography of the state.

Texas, with its current school minority population standing at nearly 50%, will become the next "minority majority" state, followed shortly by other Sun Belt states and the industrial northeast. Presently, the population of our twenty-five largest cities is made up of a majority of minority people.

Beyond these broad demographic changes, the ways in which one becomes a parent are changing too. At present, nearly fifteen percent of our children are born out of wedlock, fifty percent of those to teenage mothers. And while the economic problems associated with teenage pregnancy and childbearing have not

4

changed much in the past decade or two, the acceptance of this unwed mother phenomena is growing, giving America the highest teenage pregnancy rate of any industrialized nation on earth. In fact, every day in the United States, forty teenage girls -- a school bus full -- give birth to their third child. By some estimates, as many as 90% of unwed mothers keep their babies, raising them themselves or with the help of extended family members, such as parents, siblings or close friends.

In a system that sociologists call "skip-generation parenting," the childbearing woman's parents or siblings become the primary care givers as the mother must work to support herself and her baby. Thus, another group becomes engaged in parenting: grandparents and aunts and uncles. Many such children are raised in a widely extended family which may include several generations, including grandparents, aunts, uncles, and cousins who are blood relations and a number of other significant people who are unrelated either by blood or in any conventional legal way to the child.

One can also become a parent in other ways that have captured the attention of the American press and the court system. Artificial insemination using a sperm donor has enabled unmarried women to be the biological parents of their own children. The number of difficult-to-place children available for adoption, combined with a loosening of conventional restrictions on who can be a parent, has also increased the number of single parent adoptions.

These single parents are not unaware of the difficulties they face in a world that still views relationships in largely conventional ways. One single-mother-by-choice told a *Newsweek* (1990) reporter that she realizes she will have to explain the absence of a father to her young daughter. Her plan is to tell her "Families are different. There are all kinds. Ours is the kind with just a mommy." When the child realizes that she needed a father to be born, her mother says that she will tell her that her father was "a kind man who wanted to help me have her. We are grateful to him, but he's not involved in our life" (p. 44).

Among the most difficult parent arrangements, legally and in terms of conventional acceptance, are those of gay couples raising children. Estimates from the National Center for Lesbian Rights indicate that as many as two million gay mothers and fathers may be raising children who are legally theirs. In many cases, they are the children from earlier, heterosexual relationships, but some five thousand to ten thousand gay women have borne children after declaring their sexual orientation and hundreds of gay men and women have adopted children.

Most gay couples, though, describe themselves and their families as conventional in most ways, even boring. One partner in a gay male couple with two children said to a *Newsweek* reporter, "Our values are the same as those of our parents...we just happen to be two men." His partner added, "We're really quite boring...Just homebodies. We're Ozzie and Harry" (p. 39).

5

Family Relationships

Public acceptance of alternative family structures is growing. In a recent survey of 1200 adults by the Massachusetts Mutual Life Insurance Company only 22% used the legal definition when asked to define *family*: "A group of people related by blood, marriage or adoption." Three-quarters of them chose the much broader definition: "A group of people who love and care for each other."

Legislation and business practices are also catching up with these changing attitudes. San Francisco's "domestic partnership" legislation recognizes both gay and heterosexual partners as families, eligible for the legal status and employment benefits that accrue to such relationships. New York's Court of Appeals has upheld the status of a deceased gay man's long-term partner as "family," and legislation is working its way through a number of other states to grant family status to unmarried, long-term adult partners.

Both sociologists and legal experts have concluded that family has become a fluid concept. While many people lament the passing of the heterosexual, nuclear family that was prevalent in the early decades of this century, in fact most of us do not live in such households (a mother and father living with their minor children). Currently, only about a quarter of the country's 90 million households fit the model of the traditional family described above. Single parent families, widowed people, just-plain-singles, gay couples, unmarried heterosexual couples, skip-generation households...the variety of family arrangements is almost endless. And it is reasonable to expect that continuing economic and social changes will affect family structures well into the next century.

Without straying too far from conventional patterns, though, a common course of events, outlined in *Newsweek* (1990), can create a very complex arrangement in a single "family."

> The original plot goes like this: first comes love. Then comes marriage. Then comes Mary with the baby carriage. But now there's a sequel: John and Mary break up. John moves in with Sally and her two boys. Mary takes the baby, Paul. A year later Mary meets Jack, who is divorced with three children. They get married. Paul, barely two years old, now has a mother, a father, a stepmother, a stepfather, and five stepbrothers and stepsisters -- as well as four sets of grandparents (two biological, two step) and countless aunts and uncles. And guess what? Mary's pregnant again. (p. 24)

As many as one-third of all children born in the 1980s will live in a stepfamily or "reconstituted" or "blended" family before they reach the age of 18. Nearly 9 million children, or about 15% of all school-age children, currently live in such a family.

6

The effect of stepfamily membership on children has drawn a great deal of research attention in the past several years, and more is coming to be known about children in these situations. Not surprisingly, children living in stepfamilies share psychological and behavioral similarities with children in single-parent families, even though they are living in two-parent arrangements. Indeed, one of the most consistent findings in all of this research is that stepfamilies do not recreate the nuclear family.

Parent-child relationships are different between biological parent-child dyads and stepparent-child dyads. Most of the "parenting," including discipline, school relations, medical decisions, and other discretionary behavior, is done by the biological parent. In fact, in some institutions, the schools often being one, information is shared only with the biological parent or legal guardian. Ironically, the stepparent who has lived with a child for a long period of time may have no legal standing with him or her, but a biological parent who lives in another state and has never seen the child does have legal rights to affect the child's life.

In general, the picture of "Yours, Mine and Ours" perpetuated in the movies of happily blended families whose only conflict occurs when one family's dog chases the other family's cat up a suburban tree is a myth. Unfortunately, the desirability of that image is so strong that many people in blended families become discouraged when their problems surpass the media's version of what things are supposed to look like.

Family blending is stressful. Non-biological parents are uncertain of their roles with their "instant children." Stepchildren are unsure of their relationship to this new adult who suddenly has rights in their biological parent's life. New siblings may clash over long-established behaviors, tolerated in one family, but not by the other. Differences in scholastic ability, athletic prowess, artistic talent, social grace, popularity or peer group membership may also be a source of severe distress for newly blended siblings as well. Events become even more complicated if the new couple has a biological child of their own. Often, step children feel like outsiders in this new nuclear family, and resent the loss of their own status with their biological parent.

Conclusion

Most families, however fluid that definition has become, are simply doing what is necessary to adapt and survive in a rapidly changing environment. Thus, conventional notions of the family as a moral entity as well as a social one may hinder the efforts of public institutions to serve their clients well. To judge one kind of family structure as "right" and another as "wrong" creates a distance between the institution and its clients that makes it impossible to work effectively with them. Further, attributing all of a child's behavior to the family structure in which he lives does a great disservice to that child and undermines the school's ability to educate him or her effectively. The kid comes to the school from the only family he or she has. Judging it as the "right" or "wrong" family structure does little to advance the child's success or that of the school.

CHAPTER TWO

The Family As Educator

The importance of the family in education is such a widely accepted notion that it is almost trivial to restate it. Indeed, one group of researchers argue that it is, perhaps, the most important non-instructional influence on student performance in school (Steinberg, et al., 1989). However, as education has become more institutionalized and specialized, the participation of the family in the education of their children has been eroded by the growth of "teaching technology," or the belief that there is a very specific approach to teaching and, if it is not correctly applied, real damage will be done to the child. Parental views of education have become akin to their views of medicine: the application of the technology is best left to the experts.

At the same time, though, the literature on human learning makes it abundantly clear that significant parental participation in a child's education greatly enhances the likelihood of successful learning. After all, the parents are the ones who taught the kid the really hard stuff: like walking and language and community values. And it is no less true that parental participation will enhance academic learning as well, particularly in the areas of literacy, school attitudes, and general knowledge. In *The Evidence Continues to Grow* Anne Henderson (1987) summarizes the effects of family participation in education quite succinctly. She writes:

1. The family provides the primary educational environment.

2. Involving parents in their children's formal education improves student achievement.

3. Parent involvement is most effective when it is comprehensive, long-lasting, and well-planned.

4. The benefits [of parent involvement] are not confined to early childhood or the elementary level; there are strong

9

effects from involving parents continuously throughout high school.

5. Involving parents in their own children's education at home is not enough. To ensure the quality of schools as institutions serving the community, parents must be involved in all levels of the school.

6. Children from low-income and minority families have the most to gain when schools involve parents. Parents do not have to be well-educated to help.

7. We cannot look at the school and the home in isolation from one another; we must see how they interconnect with each other and with the world at large. (p. 9f)

Few educators would argue with any of these conclusions, drawn from Henderson's analysis of forty-nine of the most important studies on home-school participation. However, the questions to be answered are still formidable, as Henderson indicates:

1. What type and intensity of parent involvement is needed to raise the achievement level of low-income and minority children to that expected for middle class students?

2. What forms of parent involvement are most appropriate for students in middle school, junior high school and high school?

3. What resources do parents and educators need to be able to work effectively as partners?

4. What are the appropriate roles for government agencies at the federal, state and local levels in encouraging, nurturing, and expanding parental involvement?

5. What contributions can be made by others in the community, such as local service agencies, employers, business and industry, to help families and schools work better together? (p. 10)

Despite these lingering questions, it is clear that the benefits to be gained from parent involvement are worth the effort it takes. Students who graduate from schools with strong parent involvement perform better than students from identical programs without strong parental participation. Schools that are connected to their communities produce students who outperform those from schools which are isolated from their communities. (Henderson, 1987) And, most important, the long-term effects of early parental involvement are quite profound. One study indicated that high school seniors from poor families who had attended <u>preschool</u> programs with high parental involvement outperformed students who came from preschools with low parental participation. The effects of that early participation established a pattern of achievement that persisted for over twelve years! (Lazar, 1978) Few educational interventions have such a lasting effect on student achievement.

Beyond these general conclusions, though, consensus breaks down on what kind of parent involvement is needed, whether it is best delivered at home or in the school, or, indeed, just what parent involvement actually <u>is</u>. Joyce Epstein (1989) offers a useful model for thinking about parent involvement in a child's education. She theorizes that there are five different types of involvement, and, as in any hierarchical system, it is virtually impossible to promote the higher levels of involvement if the lower ones are not adequately addressed. She identifies the five types of involvement as follows:

> **Type 1.** <u>The basic obligations of parents</u>. These are the basic responsibilities associated with childrearing. They include providing for the child's health and safety, the provision of adequate guidance and discipline, and the ensuring of home conditions that support school learning, ranging from such basics as ensuring attendance to more advanced levels such as providing reasonable study facilities at home.

> **Type 2.** <u>The basic obligations of schools</u>. Basic school obligations are, generally, to communicate with the home about the school's program, the student's progress or any special needs the child may have. It includes standardized forms of communication (report cards, newsletters, etc.) as well as more individualized forms (notes home, parent-teacher conferences, etc.).

> **Type 3.** <u>Parent involvement in school</u>. This level refers to actual parent presence in the school, working as volunteers in tutorial programs, as library aides, or in other academic areas. It may also include parent management of sporting events or other activities for recreation or fund-raising, or workshops and seminars for their own training and education.

> **Type 4.** <u>Parent involvement in learning activities at home</u>. This form of participation refers to parent participation in schoolwork the child carries home, either at the child's request or that of the school. Often it involves simply answering questions or rehearsing a child for a test; other times, it is guided by specific learning activities provided by the teacher and which are coordinated with the child's classwork.

Type 5. <u>Parent involvement in governance and advocacy</u>. This level of participation involves parental leadership in PTA/PTO organizations, advisory councils, or other policy or governance groups at the school, district, state or national level. Often, this type of involvement is managed by community activist groups who monitor the school and work for improvement.

As Epstein points out, each of these types of involvement have different goals, require very different types of structures and processes, and result in very different types of outcomes. Thus, it is not enough to say that a school solicits "parent involvement." It is critical that schools plan for <u>specific</u> kinds of involvement based on the goals they are trying to achieve.

Family Effects on Student Success

A number of studies have examined the pattern of single family households and their effects on school performance. Some have identified that single parent structure was associated with lower achievement, and others have found that it is not possible to sort out the effects of single parent structures from other important variables, such as class, income, race, and amount of time available for child rearing. In general, the studies that identify single parent family structure as affecting school performance lump all kinds of single parent families together and do not consider the effects of other factors that influence the quality of life for the child, such as the existence of extended family or other support systems. (Henderson, et al., 1987)

In summarizing the research on single parent families, Anne Henderson says, "the research on single parent families is probably most useful to educators when it points out the dangers of stereotyping, to ascribing poor school performance to the single fact that the child's parents do not live in the same household. A more useful inquiry is "What are the circumstances that allow children from single parent or low income, minority homes to succeed?" (Henderson, et al., p. 108)

Additional research on the effects of maternal employment point out even more clearly the pitfalls of single variable studies. Most important is the effect of maternal employment on family income and school performance. For poor children, maternal employment is positively associated with school achievement, but the same is not necessarily true for more affluent children. The effects also seem to be different for boys and girls, with boys being somewhat more negatively affected by maternal employment and girls being more positively influenced. (Kamerman and Hayes, 1983) And in two studies, it was demonstrated that working mothers actually spend as much time at home with their children on school-related activities as do nonworking parents. (Medrich, 1982 and Epstein, 1983)

It is clear that generalizations about either the number of parents in the home or the employment patterns of parents are inappropriate at this stage of the research agenda. More complex investigations are needed to identify the effects of parenting strategies, independent of single or dual parenthood, the economic security produced by a working mother's income, and the ways in which family processes are altered by other variables, such as the quality of before and after school experiences, to produce effects on student school performance.

Thus, the most important of the recent findings on family involvement in education is the gradual decline of the notion that structural characteristics of the family affect student academic performance. Structural characteristics that have been examined in some detail are the size of the family, the number of parents present, the birth order of children, family spacing, the employment and economic status of the family, and a host of others that are often well beyond influence of the school. It is encouraging to note that, while structural characteristics seem to increase the likelihood of certain kinds of family attitudes, behavior or activity, it is the attitude, activity, or the behavior itself that affects school performance. Therefore, the family circumstances that affect education are somewhat more alterable than they would be if it were the structural features that dominated student performance. In other words, family process variables have a greater influence on student performance than do family background variables. (Linney and Vernberg, 1983)

In a foundational study of parental involvement, Reginald Clark (1983) identified patterns of family interaction that seemed to distinguish high achieving children from low achievers. Five general themes structure his conclusions: family theme and background, early child-rearing and family practices, mental health, home living patterns, and intellectuality at home.

Clark's (1983) findings indicate a number of specific family characteristics and behaviors common to the families of high-achieving minority and high-risk children:

1. Frequent school contact initiated by the parent.

2. Child has some stimulating, supportive school teachers.

3. Parents are emotionally and psychologically calm with the child.

4. Students are psychologically and emotionally calm with the parents.

5. Parents expect to play a major role in child's schooling.

6. Parents expect child to play a major role in child's schooling.

7. Parents expect child to get post-secondary training.

8. Parents have explicit achievement-centered rules and norms.

9. Students show long-term acceptance of norms as legitimate.

13

10. Parents establish clear, specific role boundaries and status structures with the parent as dominant authority.

11. Siblings interact as organized subgroup.

12. Conflict between family members is infrequent.

13. Parents frequently engage in deliberate achievement-training activities.

14. Parents frequently engaged in implicit achievement-training activities.

15. Parents exercise firm, consistent monitoring and rules enforcement.

16. Parents provide liberal nurturance and support.

17. Parents defer to child's knowledge in intellectual matters.

From the foregoing list, it is evident that family influence on school achievement is the result of specific family behaviors, rather than family structural or demographic characteristics. As a result of Clark's seminal findings, it is also clear that schools can encourage these behaviors and, thereby, increase the potential for achievement among youth from families that have been traditionally underserved by schools.

Family Involvement in Schools
The dramatic effect that family participation has on school achievement is well-documented. Virtually all of the relevant studies indicate that there is a strong "curriculum of the home," manifested in conversations, daily routines, attention to school matters, concern for their children's progress, and recreational and leisure activities, that can enhance or impede school performance. (DiPrete, 1981; Graue and others, 1983; Gray, 1984; Walberg, 1984a, 1984b)

Less clear, though, is the extent to which the parents of disadvantaged students employ the same approaches as middle class families in facilitating the achievement of their children.

White, middle-class family practices may be idiosyncratic to that group because of the close value and goal congruence between such homes and mainstream educational institutions. Less insight is currently available about the practices in poor, minority households that encourage school success.

One of the most significant lessons taught in the home is learning the value of work and steady employment. Wilson's (1987) analysis of the urban underclass identifies the disabling effects of intergenerational poverty on the job aspirations and school performance of children. He argues that joblessness is linked directly to school performance in ghetto neighborhoods:

14

...in such neighborhoods the chances are overwhelming that children will seldom interact on a sustained basis with people who are employed or with families that have a steady breadwinner. The net effect is that joblessness, as a way of life, takes on a different meaning; the relationship between schooling and postschool employment takes on a different meaning. The development of cognitive, linguistic and other educational and job-related skills necessary for the world of work in the mainstream economy is thereby adversely affected. (p. 57)

The result of pervasive joblessness, open lawlessness and low performing schools in the ghetto is that these communities tend to be avoided by outsiders. Therefore, the members of these communities have become increasingly isolated from mainstream patterns of behavior, and, in fact, discourage the presence of middle and working class families in the urban ghetto. The removal of this "buffer" has led to the decline of other basic institutions (churches, schools, stores, recreational facilities) that would have remained viable if there had been a more economically stable supporting constituency. (Wilson, 1987)

It is difficult to imagine how norms of school achievement can be fostered in an environment such as that described by Wilson. But Clark (1985) suggests that these norms and values may be transmitted by families in ways that mediate the environmental effects of the urban ghetto.

Clark found that the families of high achieving minority students possessed a strong intellectual ethos that raised learning and schooling to a profound level of awareness in the household. This intellectual ethos could be characterized as having a strong moral code and standard in the household: both sacred and secular moral codes are highly developed in high achieving disadvantaged students. Family norms, rules and expectations took the form of achievement demands that were discussed, linked to specific outcomes and generally understood by the child. Parent attitudes toward knowledge acquisition were characterized by the willingness to put the child's growth and development before their own. (The concept of parents making a sacrifice for the child's education was a strong theme recognized by children in all of Clark's families.) Parents also saw a responsibility for helping the children develop both general knowledge and special literacy skills, for encouraging of the student's pursuit of knowledge, and regularly discussing their belief that the child will participate in some form of secondary and post-secondary training.

High achieving families also tended to have a process of deliberate instruction in the home. Children were rehearsed on how to handle teacher-pupil relationships, homework and study were regular, almost ritualized, activities in the home, and home lessons were taught as the opportunity arose in daily life. Implicit pedagogy also pervaded the homes of high achieving students, consisting of games and recreational activities that related to improved school performance, including light reading and discussions about mutual experiences (such as television shows).

The families of high achieving minority students had specific social contacts with the schools. They had concerns over the school's success (or lack thereof) and, while they thought it was possible to get a good education in the neighborhood school, they did not think it was likely without parental input. Because of this belief, these parents were likely to visit the school, intermittently, to check on their child's progress and the performance of the school.

Other earlier studies establish a similar profile for the high achieving student. Dave (1963) linked parent press for achievement, parents' use of language models in the home, degree of parents' academic guidance, the quality of family routine activities, the intellectual atmosphere of the home and the division of labor in the family to children's performance in academic subjects. Wolf (1964) found that three categories of family life (parental press for achievement, parents' emphasis upon language development, and provisions for general learning in the home) were linked to measures of "intelligence." In neither of these studies was family intactness or structure related to student achievement.

Weiss (1969) found that the family sub-environment for achievement motivation had three components: nature of parent-generated standards for excellence and achievement, independence training for children, and parental support and approval of children's accomplishments. These components were significantly related to children's motivation and self-esteem.

Early research on the subject shows that virtually any kind of parent involvement in the school boosts student achievement. This is particularly true in minority and low-income schools. (Henderson, 1981; Moles, 1982; Linney, 1983; Zerchykov, 1985)

More recently, the term "parent involvement" has been clarified somewhat, allowing for more precise examinations of its effects. Henderson has distinguished two types of parent involvement that are particularly interesting to school people. The first is the kind of parent activity that is designed to improve the overall school program, without, necessarily, directly affecting the parent's own child. In general, this kind of activity includes volunteer work, involvement in school governance or advisory programs, or service in parent-teacher organizations. The second is the type of parent activity that is aimed directly at assisting one's own child, such as coming to teacher conferences, helping with assignments, or attending school events.

As reported earlier, regardless of the type of activity, the most beneficial effects come from carefully planned participation from the earliest grades of schooling, reinforced throughout the school experiences that are shared by the parent and the child, and continuing through middle level school and high school.

Student improvements were most noticeable in cases where parents participated intensely and over a long period of time in both types of activity: that directed at general benefit to the school, and that associated with help for their own child.

At the secondary level, less is known about family involvement. However, the research shows promising trends. In a study of 20 high schools, the critical variable in both student achievement and in their aspiration levels was the extent and nature of parent and community interest in quality education. Thus, something as abstract as a strong community/parent value regarding the importance of education affected student performance. (McDill, 1969) Later studies (NCES, 1985) show that high school parent involvement and interest is a significant factor in student success. Regardless of race, family structure or economic class, students whose parents monitored both their academic performance and their leisure time whereabouts did significantly better in school than students not so monitored.

The nature of this involvement ranges from direct assistance with school studies to participation in school events (such as parent night, athletic and artistic events, parent education programs) to the sharing of family and community values associated with achievement. (Johnston, 1989) In a recent study, children whose parents performed well in school recalled parental stories about the parents' own achievements, or how they turned a failure into an opportunity. Among lower achieving children, the recalled parental stories focussed on unfairness, failure, and unresolved school difficulty, including disciplinary actions taken against them. (Johnston, 1989)

Parental involvement in governance and advocacy has less clearly defined effects on student school performance. First, the nature and quality of parental participation in governance varies widely, and is largely a function of the amount of support and encouragement given by the principal. (Foster, 1984) In addition, many parental participation programs fail to exert much influence on the school because parents are either poorly trained for their roles or have a single agenda they wish to pursue, ignoring other critical aspects of school success and failure. (Lyons, 1982)

There is evidence, however, that parent involvement in the governance and advocacy function can have real pay-offs for students. Recently, James Comer (1988) has identified positive academic outcomes associated with parental involvement in school governance. Furthermore, his research adds to the long established body of evidence that schools with strong parental participation in governance and advocacy also have high levels of other kinds of parent involvement. (Zerchykov, 1985)

Conclusions

The variety of forms that parent involvement in schooling takes makes it difficult to understand the precise outcomes that result from it. However, the evidence is clear that both school-sponsored involvement and parent-initiated contacts with the school are linked to improved school performance and student achievement. At its most fundamental level, parent involvement appears to communicate a set of values to the children in the school: "education is important and we will cooperate with the school to see that you succeed."

CHAPTER THREE

Barriers To Home-School Cooperation

Conflict between families and schools is inevitable. Dissimilarities between the two institutions result from both their structural properties and their cultural purposes and produce difficulties that are experienced by all children as they move from home to school. (Lightfoot, 1978)

In families, the interactions are functionally diffuse. All of the participants are intimately connected to one another, and membership in the family unit is a given...a birthright. The rights and duties of this membership are all-encompassing, governing even the smallest details of life.

Schools, on the other hand, are functionally specific. That is, memberships and relationships are "defined by the technical competence and individual status of the participants" (Dreeben,1968). Thus, while attendance is required of all children, full, participating membership in the school group is largely dependent upon performance and competence. More specifically, student status and membership, and therefore relationships, are determined by performance and competence as judged by the teacher.

From these perspectives come differing expectations for children from each institution. Parents have particular expectations of children (Tina does this...) and schools have universal expectations of children (Children do this...).

Particularistic expectations take into account the individual qualities of a child, "making allowances" for special needs or developmental conditions. Universalistic expectations are of such global nature that they are applied to the entire group. They are explicit, public and, presumably, objective. (McPherson, 1972; Getzels, 1974)

As Lightfoot (1978) points out, the manifestations of these different expectations are clear even at the semantic level. So, when a parent asks a teacher to be "fair" to her child, to give him "a chance," she is really saying that she wants her child to be given special attention -- some special consideration of an individual quality that affects school performance. In other words, "fair" means "give him a break." When the teacher replies that she is being "fair" to all of the children, she means that she is "giving equal amounts of attention, judging every one by the same...standard and using explicit and public criteria for making judgments" (Lightfoot, 1978). She is treating everyone the same way, or "fairly." This contrast between the primary relationship of parent and child and the secondary relationship of teacher and child is created, in practice, by the fact that parents have emotionally charged relationships with their children that are not found in institutions, such as schools, which determine membership and status on the basis of functional performance.

The doctrine of fairness exercised in schools, therefore, strikes most parents as anything but fair to their child. But, from the school's point of view, that doctrine produces the rationality, order, and predictability so highly prized by bureaucratic institutions. For parents, though, this rational order is experienced essentially as institutional detachment from the unique and special needs of their child. From that, they conclude that the institution prizes its order more than its clients, and the seeds of distrust are sown.

As conceived and organized, schools do not perform or extend the nurturant-learning function played by the family. Because the schools are public institutions, with allegiance to the public weal and the public order, the nature of relationships between teachers and children reflects "the preparatory, transitional and sorting functions of schools in this society. The roles allocated to children in school are evaluated primarily in terms of their contributions to some future status rather than reflecting full membership in the present society" (Lightfoot, 1978).

Bowles and Gintis (1976) are considerably more pointed in describing the effects of this phenomenon on minority students, saying that consignment to an inner city school helps assure the continued economic subordination of minorities. Specifically, students in inner city schools are discouraged from developing levels of self-esteem, intellectual performance, and personal competence that future employers are likely to regard as indicators of promise or ability. Instead, disadvantaged workers were inclined to report that "appearance" was more important to potential employers than test scores, previous work history or academic diplomas or awards. (Bowles and Gintis, 1976)

Furthermore, schools adopt behavioral norms that reflect the future social position of their students. Schools with large concentrations of poor and minority students exhibit control mechanisms, treatment of students and intellectual demands that are very different from predominantly white schools.

Blacks and minorities are concentrated in schools
whose repressive, arbitrary, generally chaotic internal

order, coercive authority structures and minimal possibilities for advancement mirror the characteristics of inferior job situations. Similarly, predominantly working-class schools tend to emphasize behavioral control and rule following, while schools in well-to-do suburbs employ relatively open systems which favor greater student participation, less direct supervision, more electives and in general a value system stressing internalized standards of control. (Bowles and Gintis, 1976, p. 132)

Thus, in middle class schools, students are rewarded for individuality, aggressiveness and initiative. In poor schools, students were reinforced for passivity, behavioral compliance, withdrawal and obedience (Leacock, 1969).

Schools' View of Families

As a matter of practice, the boundaries between school and home are relatively ambiguous. Parents and the school argue about who is "in control" during school time; indeed, they argue about what "school time" actually is. Does the parent have the right to keep a child home from school for reasons other than illness? Can a teacher keep a child after school for extra work or punishment? While parents and teacher often disagree over the right to control certain aspects of the child's life, public policy and legal precedent generally side with the parent. (Lightfoot, 1978)

One domain that is clearly the teacher's is the classroom. There is a long tradition of professional autonomy in schools, provided such autonomy is enacted in the confines of one's own classroom. "Behind the classroom door, teachers experience some measure of autonomy and relief from parental scrutiny, and parents often feel, with shocking recognition, the exclusion and separation from their child's world" (Lightfoot, 1978). The territoriality that drives this separation comes, largely, from the ambiguous assignment of authority and responsibility for the children. This ambiguity is exacerbated by the distrust produced by the structural discontinuities outlined above, and remains unresolved because there are virtually no opportunities for parents and teachers to meet for meaningful discussions about competence, roles and responsibilities. Generally, parent and school contact is much too ritualized for true role negotiation to take place.

The public rituals organized by schools (Open House, Parent Night, etc.) do not permit real contact or discussion. In fact, they tend to showcase the very artifacts of "unfairness" that earn the parents' distrust in the first place, such as grades, rules, school programs and school policies...evidence that the institutional order is more important than the individual child and his learning. When the parent fails to participate in these rituals, however, the judgment of the school is that they are "disinterested" in their child's education, or, worse, openly hostile to the school and its purposes. As Warren (1973) points out, these school rituals simply reaffirm the "idealized parent-school relationship" but seldom permit any form of useful dialogue. Parents and teachers are unwilling to risk public exposure at these meetings by raising private problems ("Why isn't my child doing more reading?"), and parents fear that an aggressive, outspoken style might engender a negative reaction toward their child by the school.

Individual contacts between parents and teachers are rare, and are generally called because of dissatisfaction, frustration or anger on the part of the parent or teacher. Citing conversations with a city teacher, Lightfoot and Carew (1974) quote the following:

> When we call parents during the year, it's generally
> to say that your child is being disruptive or your child
> seems sad. Is there something the matter at home? Your
> child has been talking about some problem. Is it true?

When these interactions become heated, difficult or irresolvable, the school demonstrates its power with additional experts in the form of counselors, psychologists or administrators. In fact, nearly forty years ago, Becker (1952) noted the balance of forces in Chicago's inner-city schools. Teachers and administrators unified for mutual protection against interference by parents. Citing Becker, Lightfoot (1978) notes that "Teachers made an implicit bargain with their superiors that they would support the organization as long as the organization served to protect them from...critics" (p. 29).

The likelihood of conflict between teachers and the parents of disadvantaged children runs particularly high. Majority teachers have little familiarity with the development and behavior of minority children, especially males, primarily because there is so little firsthand contact between the races. (Hale-Benson, 1982) As a result, they tend to view the masculinity rituals of black males as disruptive, insolent or confrontational.

Worse, though, is the more insidious ethnocentricism found in much behavioral science research (on which the vast majority of teachers are trained) which accepts the development of white children as the norm. To illustrate, Hale-Benson (1982) cites studies from the 1950s which showed black infants to have more advanced sensorimotor skills than white infants. In this case, the white infants were not classified as "developmentally delayed" or "retarded," the black infants were simply labeled "precocious." Thus, she says, the "notion of white normality is maintained" (p. 180).

Stereotypic views of disadvantaged families are deeply embedded in school wisdom. With virtually no firsthand contact with minority families, without any mechanism for securing their point of view, schools have developed very strong perceptions of the family that serve to justify its exclusion from the schooling process. Lightfoot (1978) explains, "one of the predominant myths about black parents and poor parents...is that they do not care about the education of their children, are passive and unresponsive to attempts by teachers and administrators to get them involved, and are ignorant and naive about the intellectual and social needs of their children" (p. 36). As outlined in the next section, nothing could be further from the truth.

Family Views of the School

The view that education is a vehicle for mobility is widely held in the minority community, and clearly documented in the literature on family life and school achievement. Hylan Lewis found that "the added value placed on education of black children as a means of escaping low and achieving high status is a myth-like cultural theme" (Lewis, 1967, p. 400). In his study of urban neighborhoods, John Ogbu (1974) reported distinct norms and values about achievement and the utility of schooling as a vehicle for success. In fact, it may be those very values that create difficulties in the black community. Lewis indicates that it may well be the very high parental aspirations for disadvantaged children, when confronted with the real, social and economic limitations on their opportunities, that invites disruptive behavior in their children.

How can disadvantaged families keep their faith in education in the face of such overwhelming evidence that it does not provide much mobility for their children? Lightfoot (1978) explains, "Although our rational minds tell us that there is no evidence of group mobility for blacks through schooling, we know the stories of individual mobility -- perhaps we ourselves are the proud products of social and economic advancement through schooling. Our heroes keep that image alive" (p. 126).

Poor parents often feel that they can do little but turn their children over to the school, the institution which arbitrates success and mobility, and hope for the best. Otherwise, their exclusion from the process of educating their children is quite nearly complete. Lightfoot (1978) says "they lose control of their child's daily life, as someone else becomes the expert and judge of their child's abilities, and as they are perceived as interlopers, unwelcome intruders..." Thus, parents come to see themselves as powerless to affect their child's school experience. They learn that they are not teachers, and that they can do little to help their child succeed in school.

Our schools operate on the edge of an "experiential chasm" that separates children from their parents. (Slater, 1968) This distance between what the parents have experienced and the children are experiencing (in school or in their daily lives) serves to undermine the child's perception of parental wisdom and lessens the parents' ability to participate in education which is oriented toward the future. For poor and minority parents, the combination of this generational chasm with the isolation from their child's school experience undermines their confidence that they can indeed understand what their child is learning and, in fact, help him with it.

Beyond this gulf, parents must also cope with their own recalled school experiences in dealing with their child's school. For many poor parents, their own school experiences were unsuccessful and disabling. And when they approach the institution, it is often with images of a tyrannical, authoritarian teacher figure that is projected onto the teachers of their children. Often, parents do not see teachers as potential collaborators, but as arbitrary and capricious authority figures. (Lightfoot, 1978)

23

More recent studies (Leitch and Tangri, 1988), though, have indicated that parents' poor school experiences may be less influential than first thought. Most of the parents interviewed in these investigations indicated that they liked school pretty well even if their academic performance was not strong. Even those who reported poor school performance tended to ascribe it to lack of motivation and interest, either a flaw they saw in themselves or a difficulty they ascribed to an individual school, not to schooling in general.

In either case, though, the outcome is quite similar: parents do not see themselves as able contributors to their child's success. In these cases, anything less than direct and sustained efforts by the school to overcome that feeling and encourage and support parent involvement is likely to reinforce their detachment from the schooling process. Simply leaving the door open for parental involvement isn't enough. The school must usher parents through that door.

Conclusion

It is clear that effective schooling is difficult without parent support and nearly impossible if parents hold hostile attitudes toward the school. To a large degree, though, neither parents nor schools have a very profound understanding of the character of the other institution. In fact, in a recent study (Johnston, 1989) teachers responded differently to questions about school practices when they were asked to think about their effects on their students and their families than when they were asked to think about the effects of the same practice on their own children and themselves if it were employed by their own child's school.

Schools must take the initiative in building meaningful bridges between the home and the school, for it is the school that realizes just how essential parent participation is for a child's success. Not only must opportunities be given, but genuine invitations must be extended for important kinds of participation.

CHAPTER FOUR

Involving Families In Schooling

Beyond the normal responsibilities of parenting, to feed, clothe, house and otherwise secure their child's environment, there are three avenues available to parents for participation in their child's education. They can support their child's educational efforts through indirect and direct participation at home, such as achievement training, the transmittal and shaping of attitudes that support education, and specific assistance with schoolwork. They can also participate in the child's schooling, either in ways that directly influence children, such as tutoring or monitoring student behavior, or in ways that benefit the school in general, such as volunteer work in more generalized functions, such as library-media services, food services, or clerical service. Finally, they can participate in the formation of school policies and practices through participation in some form of governance activity, either through a recognized leadership position, or by supporting one of the ancillary organizations, such as the PTA/PTO or a community council, that has recognized status in the governance system of the school or district.

Each of these forms of participation depends upon the school's willingness to involve parents and its skill in managing their own practices so that parental involvement is actually encouraged rather than discouraged. In this section, school practices in three areas will be proposed to enhance parent participation: awareness of family variety, services to families, and provision for governance or other school participation by families.

Awareness
The greatest weapon that school reformers have is the abiding good will and compassion for children that is shared by the vast majority of our professional educators and other school staff. Often, simple awareness of a problem is sufficient to engage these well-intentioned people in searching for solutions for it. Thus, the first step in making the middle level school "family friendly" is to raise awareness about the incredible diversity that exists in family composition in the school and the effects that standard school practices might have on those

nontraditional families. A key to raising this awareness is to focus attention on school practices that affect family life, rather than upon making judgments about what is or should be "normal" family behavior.

Whenever a major new construction project is planned, both Federal Law and common sense dictate that an "environmental impact statement" be prepared in order to assess the probable effect of the project on the vicinity in which it will be located. A similar mind-set is useful in thinking about how school practices affect families.

As a normal part of the school change process, two questions should be raised:

> "What effect will this new requirement, policy, or process have on the various types of families in this community?"

> "Does this new policy, process or material discriminate against any particular type of family group?"

Generally, simply raising the question will assure that new practices are scrutinized from the point of view of the client families served by the school. Similar discussions should be held in departmental meetings or team meetings to determine the likely effects of certain instructional interventions that might be planned. And it is not unreasonable to expect individual teachers to ask these same questions about any proposed assignment or requirement that may be unique to that teacher's classroom.

Several examples serve to illustrate how even relatively innocuous practices can create hardships for certain types of families. In one case, an adopted child was given the popular assignment to "trace his family tree" and report on when his ancestors immigrated to the United States and from which country they came. However, this child had entered the US as a refugee from an orphanage in a Central American country. When he asked his parents what to do, they suggested that he use their family tree, since he was, indeed, a member of that family. In school the next day, each child reported on the immigration status of his or her family. When it came to Carlos, the teacher wrote his very Hispanic sounding last name on the board only to be told that his family arrived from Ireland...in 1908. The teacher replied, "With a last name like yours, you certainly can't have an Irish family!" To which Carlos said, "I don't know who my biological parents are...but I do have an Irish family."

That example is not a shattering experience, but it does illustrate how innocent remarks can convey to a student that he is somehow not "normal." And if the school tells me I'm quite different from everyone else around here, and makes me feel different often enough, I'll soon stop looking to the school as a source of affiliation, satisfaction, and reward. Imagine how much worse this

26

scenario could have been if the child's parents were in the United States illegally, or if he lived in a foster home, or with gay parents, or with an unmarried couple who had no biological or legal relationship to him. It would have been so much safer to change the assignment only slightly...to "trace the family tree of a family you know about. It might be your own, or someone else you know." Such a minor change would provide the kind of psychic distance that shelters our children from unnecessary judgments about the normality of their particular family circumstances.

Other examples are somewhat more complicated and involve legal definitions. In one case, a girl was suspended from school for swearing at a teacher in a fit of anger. Almost everyone in the school agreed it was a first offense, but the rules were quite specific about the punishment: she could not return until her parents came with her. Her father was incarcerated, her mother was in a drug addiction rehabilitation program. She lived with her grandmother and the man who shared her grandmother's home. Because neither had legal authority to act as her "parent," she was denied re-entry into the school. Only the beneficial intervention of a judge, who recognized that this "family" was constituted out of compassion and a need to help out the girl's parents, not out of law, allowed the girl to return to school. The problem was fixed, but imagine, for a moment, what it feels like to come back to a place which had to be compelled to re-admit you with a court order.

As a first step, schools should undertake a "family impact assessment" of their curriculum, rules, practices and policies. Do fee policies keep certain kinds of children from participating in school events? Does the lack of child care keep parents away from school activities? Do special assignments to be done at home, such as for science projects, or craft fairs, or art shows, assume a certain type of Ozzie and Harriet family, one with ample resources for materials and enough time and expertise to help the child succeed?

One school makes a practice of devoting a portion of their faculty meetings to a discussion of the kinds of problems that have come to their attention when the school's program intersects with the normal lives of their students' families. In many cases, such a discussion encourages teachers to step out of their professional roles and think about how a given practice in their school might affect them as a parent. Indeed, many teachers do have children in their schools and have a special opportunity to share information about the effects of school practices with their colleagues.

Another middle level school goes a step further. One evening a year they invite a panel of their parents to address the faculty on issues that concern them. This panel is selected by the PTO and the local teacher's union. The purpose is to let the teachers hear, first hand, what some of the problems are that parents face in dealing with the school. Often, the panel contains a local teacher. In virtually every case, the discussion has focussed exclusively on <u>practices</u> (from homework to cheerleading) not personalities, and the result is that a useful and mutually supportive dialogue is opened on vital issues.

In what may be the most formal manifestation of a school's commitment to families, a big-city middle school has a local parent advisory panel that reviews virtually every policy change and many of the school practices on a routine basis. These parents also routinely survey and interview other parents associated with the school, attempting to identify issues that affect their connection with the school. This outreach, coupled with a very responsive administration and staff, has created a tradition of quality customer service in this school that marks it as a leader in community relations. Furthermore, the students' performance on most conventional measures of success (grades, test scores, attendance, awards, drop out rates) outshines virtually every other school in the area.

Services

Schools are a major service provider to the American public. Some do it better than others, but the expectation of the public is that schools are a service institution.

To a large extent, this orientation reflects the growing consumerism among American families, and a growing willingness to compete for customers on the part of agencies both in the private and the public sectors. Even other monopolies, such as utility companies, recognize that service to their clients, even though they generally have no alternative, pays off for the utility as well. Good consumer relations lead to less litigation, less regulation by external forces, and better service and profitability. Thus, it is important for schools to begin thinking about the nature and quality of service they offer the public, not only to benefit the customers but, in so doing, to benefit the school and its employees as well. The kinds of service that schools can offer depend largely on the clientele they serve and can range from programs that are intimately connected to the schools' central purpose, such as providing a homework assistance hotline, to services that are somewhat less traditionally found in schools, such as crisis referral services for families in difficulty. Clearly, though, the type of service offered to the community should reflect the community's needs and expectations, not, initially, what the school thinks is "good for" the community.

In general, three kinds of services are offered to families: those that are directly related to their child's schooling, those that are indirectly related to their child's schooling, and those that provide support for the family itself.

Among the services directly related to the child's schooling is a wide ranging collection indeed. These are the services that are designed to involve the parent in helping deliver the curriculum to their child.

At one level, this type of family assistance may be in the form of teacher advice to the parents on how to help children complete homework, prepare for a test, or finish a project. Beyond that, teachers may actually suggest home-based instructional activities that reinforce in-class learning. Giving parents ways of supporting specific concepts while going about normal home routines, such as meal preparation, home repairs, TV viewing or other recreation, or gardening, for example, involves the parents in meaningful ways and, at the same time, allows them to assist competently in their child's learning. Unfortunately, assignments are often seen by parents strictly as "schoolwork carried home" and many of them feel ill-prepared to help their children because they are unfamiliar with the technical aspects of the assignment. This is often the case in subjects such as math, science or foreign languages, but can also occur in areas where parents believe their own competence is weak, such as reading or writing. Linking school work to normal routines can help eliminate these feelings on the part of parents.

Information sharing may also be thought of as a service to families. Information about routine school events as well as specialized information about a parent's child are important aspects of the service that schools provide. And, as with all of its services, it is critical that this information be of the highest quality and in the most useable form.

Quite frankly, general information about the school and its programs is usually of interest to parents only if they see how it affects their child. A lengthy newsletter about the school's new science program is not likely to get much attention, unless it contains rather specific information about how it will benefit the children, how it will enhance other kinds of learning, how it conforms to community values, or how the children are reacting to it.

Furthermore, information which does not ask for some kind of parental response is often ignored. Simply announcing a parent open-house will capture the interest of those parents who are likely to come anyway. It may do little to motivate reluctant parents to attend. Instead, a short article on how to use open-house to help your child improve his or her school performance will engender more interest on the part of parents, and may help both the parent and the school focus on clear objectives for the open house or other form of school meeting that depart from the all-too-usual "show and tell" approach.

Specific information about children and their learning is highly valued by parents, provided it is balanced and useful. This information usually takes two forms: routine reports (such as mid-quarter reports, and report cards) and special contacts (such as parent conferences or notes or phone calls about a child's work or behavior).

Routine information, whether it is in written form or comes in a meeting, must meet two criteria. It must be useful and it must be understandable. Report cards and mid-quarter reports must avoid the use of jargon or vague descriptions of a child's behavior. General comments about a child ("He is not working up to his potential" or "She is not adjusting well to the class.") are often seen as judgmental. They are seldom of any use, for they give no direction on how to proceed or what the parent can do to correct the problem. It is much better to describe behavior ("Joe has missed seven out of ten homework assignments this term," or "Caroline seems to avoid contact with other students during free periods, such as lunch."). Such descriptions are emotionally neutral and encourage a parent to help interpret and explain the student's behavior. It avoids presenting the parents with a foregone conclusion about their child, one with which they can only agree or disagree. In short, it invites participation and mutual problem-solving.

Parent understanding is also critical to securing their aid. Whether it is a grade or a comment, parents must actually understand the basis on which the grade was awarded or the comment was made. Sometimes this means that communication with the home must be in the parent's language. Other times, it means that jargon-free, plain language must be used, particularly if the parents' own educational background has not prepared them to read and understand printed material very well.

In one school, each grade is "explained" by a series of comments which are selected by teachers from a computerized menu of nearly 800 such comments. Thus a student's report card in English might look like this:

> GRADE: B
> EXPLANATION OF GRADE: Student pays attention in class. Student helps other students with assignments. Student generally submits all work, but _____ assignments were not turned in this quarter. Student has good comprehension of reading material. Student demonstrates fair writing skill, and uses language cleverly in writing. Student should work on using more detail to support written work. Student should work on using standard punctuation in writing.

While the language may be a bit stilted, it does communicate to the parent the judgments on which the teacher is basing her grade. It also invites a parental response: "What can I do to help?" Finally, it outlines fairly specific actions the student can take to improve her grade. These comments can be generated, almost without limit, for each subject the student takes.

As much as parents value routine information about their child, it is the unscheduled, spontaneous contact from school that gets the most attention. Getting a note or a phone call from school about a child is still a pretty important event.

It is absolutely critical that these types of contacts be balanced: parents should hear at least as many positive comments about their child as negative ones. This means that teachers and school officials must be willing to look for praiseworthy behavior and take the time to share it with parents. This strategy accomplishes two things. It tells the parents that the school is a supportive atmosphere where their adolescent is noticed for what he or she does right. More importantly, it demonstrates to the parents that the school has a balanced view of the student, so that if it becomes necessary for the school to call the parent about

30

a difficulty, the parent and the school already have a history of recognizing the good aspects of the student's behavior and academic performance as well.

Certain practices make it easier for the school to maintain this kind of spontaneous contact with the home. First, it must be easy for the teacher to manage. A midwestern middle school gives each teacher a printout with five copies of each student's home address preprinted on address labels. At virtually any time, the teacher can quickly peel off a label, attach it to a note and drop it in the school mail. This convenience invites frequent contact with the student's home, and the printout itself helps the teacher keep track of the number of contacts she has had with the family over the course of the year. Dozens of middle level schools use "Good News Grams" of one form or another, the purpose of which is to share a bit of good news about a child with the parent. Another school places phones in each teacher's room so that calls can be made during planning periods.

It is critical that these contacts invite a parental response. The parents should be asked to comment on the news they have received, either good or bad, and be provided with a mechanism for doing so, such as a preprinted return envelope or a time when the teacher has "phone hours" and can take calls. Modern technology has also made answering machines available so that teachers can receive phone messages directly and return them at a later time.

Parent conferences are a special form of contact, for along with information exchange comes a host of other messages, many of which are non-verbal, any of which can shape the nature of the conversation between parents and teachers. Often these conferences can be emotionally charged, either by a teacher's frustration over dealing with a particularly difficult student, or by a parent's recalled poor treatment at the hands of her own teachers and school officials.

Joan Wolf and Thomas Stephens (1989) recommend that teachers spend some time building rapport with the parent and getting information from them. Simple small talk, about weather, traffic, a local event, any of those hundreds of things that adults use to make contact with one another, is appropriate at the outset. Ultimately, though, it is necessary to begin talking about the child, and these authors suggest that the parent should be invited to talk first with a question such as, "What has Carla said about her school activities?" During this phase, teachers should ask open-ended questions, rather than yes-no questions. The objective here is to get the parent talking about his or her child, and to share information that may advance the teacher's understanding of the student's school performance and behavior.

Giving information to the parents comes next. Teachers should provide descriptive information about the child's learning and behavior. Both the parent and the teacher should agree on the analysis and interpretation of this information. Finally, the conference concludes with a discussion of follow-up activities. What will the parents do? The teacher? The school? What problem or opportunities will both the home and the school focus upon? Is there to be another conference? When? What provisions are made for staying in touch with the parents?

Thinking about the conference as a systematic process eliminates some of the anxiety that often accompanies the experience. It is, after all, a conversation between adults about how to help a student succeed. Often, it is difficult to give balanced feedback to parents.

No one likes to be the bearer of bad news. To help alleviate this problem, a set of important guidelines for conducting parent conferences during which positive and negative feedback must be given is provided by Susan Swap (1987):

1. Present a balanced picture of the child, including strengths as well as problems. Also, try to identify at least one non-trivial aspect of the child that you find particularly appealing or interesting and share information about this feature with enthusiasm.

2. Give important feedback promptly.

3. Do not attempt to give feedback on a wide range of issues in a single session. Make a limited number of suggestions for improvement.

4. Try to limit feedback to something which can be changed.

5. Express the feedback in specific terms, providing examples or citing specific, observable behaviors.

6. Avoid being judgmental: describe behaviors, not what you might assume to be the motives underlying the behaviors. However, it might be productive to think together about what the possible reasons for the behaviors might be, since many variables generally shape behavior.

7. Avoid giving feedback when you are angry.

8. Avoid being so kind and tactful that you do not give the message you intend. In the long run, it is not a kindness to hedge or be wishy-washy when the outline of the problem is very clear to you. If you are not direct about your message, parents may look back later and insist that you never told them what was happening. On the

other hand, if you are not sure of what is going on, a tentative tone is very appreciated.

9. Avoid jargon or difficult technical terms.

10. Ask for and listen to reactions to the feedback you give. If appropriate, seek parents' cooperation or help in trying to resolve the problem.

In short, the parent conference should be treated as a meeting between reasonable people trying to advance a shared goal.

Other services provided by the school can provide messages about how important their parental community is to them. If the school provides child care during school events or for parent conferences, if the school sponsors a parent network that offers information about child rearing or enhancing school success for all children, or if the school provides a social setting for parents who wish to use its facilities for recreation, education or community meetings, a message is being sent that "we care about you, your child and this community. We value your participation and will do what it takes to promote it."

Parent Participation

Opportunities for parental participation in the life of the school are almost endless. They are limited only by the imaginations of the school and the community. Family members can serve as tutors, clerical aides, language instructors, career resources, "grandparents," club directors, coaches, dramatic and musical directors...the list is inexhaustible. But, for any of that to happen, certain conditions must prevail, as outlined by Dorothy Rich (1987).

1. Support family involvement as an integral and funded part of the school's services. Staff salary increases can be linked specifically to the expectation that certain home-school relations will be conduced. Home-school liaison workers can be designated from the community and appointed to paraprofessional roles, with the expectation being that they cultivate and coordinate parent involvement.

2. Provide teachers with training and information to help them work with families. Staff development activities should focus on the ways to work with families served by the school. Approaches often can be recommended by parents who work in the school or by panels of parents who are served by the school.

3. Provide for family involvement at all levels of schooling. Families should be involved not only in the early years of schooling, but throughout the child's

educational experience. Define roles for families at each level, elementary, middle and high school, and encourage different forms of participation appropriate to each level and each type of community.

4. Use school facilities for community needs. Schools should be seen not only as educators, but as an integral part of the community's social support network. Schools can provide information about social services available in the community, can act as a referral service for families in crisis, or simply become a community center during non-school hours.

5. Find ways to coordinate teacher/school schedules to the work schedules of today's families. Not only should specific school functions be scheduled to accommodate parents (such as early morning or evening parent conferences), but other opportunities should be provided for working parents to serve the school: building playground equipment, helping out with stage shows, or tutoring non-English speaking parents or children to name a very few. In short, parents should be able to participate in the life of the school even though they work during normal school hours.

Governance

Family involvement in the governance of the school can range from the use of local school advisory committees (LSAC) to more formalized governance structures, such as the local site management boards elected recently in the city of Chicago. This latter group has major power in running the school, ranging from the right to hire and fire administrators to budget and curriculum oversight responsibility. Advisory committees, on the other hand, are usually employed for advice, counsel, and liaison work with the community. In either case, the mechanisms result in shared power and ownership of the school and its programs.

Although advisory boards can operate in many ways, generally the term refers to a representative client group that meets regularly to offer advice to the school and make decisions when it is appropriate to do so. Normally, this group is convened by the school itself, although the chair often comes from outside of the institution.

Representatives to the advisory group can be elected by constituent groups (such as a PTO/PTA or teachers) selected from representative agencies in the community (a local business group or Chamber of Commerce), or other related institutions (a university, clergy group, or major employer in the community). Regardless of the process, it should yield a group of people who are interested in the school, committed to the welfare of children, unbiased, and without a specific axe to grind.

34

Advisory groups can be a disaster. If they are unfocussed or unsure of their role, they may feel that they are to manage the day-to-day affairs of the school. Almost as bad, they may feel that their job is only to launch pie-in-the-sky ideas for the school staff to implement. Ideally, the panel works to secure information, review practices and procedures, and recommend improvements where necessary, appropriate and reasonable. Susan Swap (1987) identifies some of the major questions the advisory group might address if their task were to initiate and implement a parent education program in the school:

> What programs do the parents want?

> What are their top priorities?

> Would this topic be the best choice for meeting this priority?

> Would this format and time be appropriate?

> What ideas do we have for speakers and other supporting resources?

> What reactions did the parents have to the last program?

> How can we encourage participation?

> What follow-up programs are needed?

> What long-term goals should be established?

> How can we foster better linkage between home and school?

In essence, it is clear that advisory boards are most useful in dealing with issues and programs that involve parents in some way, such as parent education or parent volunteers. They are also important in discussing issues that relate to the school program as it affects the family, as through homework, special fees, field trips, special projects and the like. Finally, they are a vital link in the community education program, and may be in an excellent position to lead newcomers (or real estate agents) on tours of the school, provide information to civic groups, or conduct studies of community attitudes or needs related to the school.

The rapidly growing trend toward the use of parent/community advisory boards points to the tremendous impact they have had on school performance and success. It has been such a powerful influence, that, in some cases, it has been institutionalized through law or policy.

In Chicago, each of the city's schools has a managing board with powers usually reserved only to the Board of Education. In New Haven, James Comer (1988), implemented a "governance and management group" in two experimental schools. This group was comprised of representatives from all the adult groups in the school, including parents, and was chaired by the principal. It developed a comprehensive building plan and worked to strengthen the relationships among all of the groups served by the school.

While the ultimate results of these projects are not yet known, it is clear that schools are responding to the research that is reported early in this document: the school cannot do it all; education is a partnership of the home, the school and the community at large.

AFTERWORD

Enough is known about the importance of family participation in education to make it a leading priority in educational reform. At the same time, schools know too little about the make-up and needs of the "New American Family" described in the first sections of this monograph. No longer, then, can parental participation be regarded solely as having parents follow recommendations that the school makes to them. Indeed, many of the recommendations that worked in the early years of this century will no longer be successful with the new family.

Instead, parental participation must be encouraged at all levels of schooling and in a wide variety of its functions. We must be prepared to learn from families what it is they need. We must be alert to the practices that disenfranchise certain kinds of families from the educational system. And, most of all, we must be mindful of our own prejudices and preconceptions about what a family really is.

Sensitive educators, working in the best interests of America's youth, almost always figure out what to do. But the absolute bottom line was expressed with simple eloquence by an aging welfare recipient who is raising the two young children of her daughter, killed by an overdose of drugs. She said, "When I send them to school all I really want those teachers to do is just be nice to them...just be nice and kind. After all, they're all I got."

REFERENCES

Becker, H. (1952). Social Class Variations in Teacher-Pupil Relationships. *Journal of Educational Sociology*, 25: 451-465.

Bowles, S. and Gintis, H. (1976). *Schooling in Capitalist America*. New York: Basic Books.

Clark, R. (1983). *Family Life and School Achievement*. Chicago: University of Chicago Press.

Clark, R. (1988). *Critical Factors in Why Disadvantaged Students Succeed or Fail in School*. Washington, DC: Academy for Educational Development.

Comer, James P. (1986). Parent Participation in the Schools. *Phi Delta Kappan*, 67:442-446, February.

Comer, James P. (1988). Is Parenting Essential to Good Teaching? *NEA Today: Issues '88*, special edition, January.

Dave, R. H. (1963). *The Identification and Measurement of Environmental Process Variables that are Related to Educational Achievement*. Ph. D. Dissertation, University of Chicago.

DiPrete, T. A. (1981). *Discipline, Order and Student Behavior in American High Schools*. Chicago: National Opinion Research Center. ERIC Document: ED 224137.

Dreeben, R. (1968). *On What is Learned In School*. Reading, MA: Addison Wesley.

English, F. W. (1988). The Utility of the Camera in Qualitative Inquiry. *Educational Researcher*, 17: 8-15, May.

Epstein, Joyce L. (1987). Parent Involvement. *Education and Urban Society*, 19:119-136, February.

Epstein, J. L. (1989). On Parents and Schools: A Conversation with Joyce Epstein. *Educational Leadership*, 47:2:24-28.

Epstein, J. L. and Becker, H. J. (1983). Teacher Reported Practices of Parent Involvement: Problems and Possibilities. *Elementary School Journal*, 83:2.

Foster, K. (March, 1984). Parent Advisory Councils: School Partners or Handy Puppets. *Principal*, 1984:27-31.

Getzels, J. W. (1974). Socialization and Education: A Note On Discontinuities. *Teachers College Record*, 76:218-225, December.

Graue, M. E, Weinstein, T. and Walberg, H. J. (1983). School-based Home Instruction and Learning: A Quantitative Synthesis. *Journal of Educational Research*, 76:351-360.

Gray, S. T. (1984). How to Create a Successful School-Community Partnership. *Phi Delta Kappan*, 65: 405-409.

Hale-Benson, J. E. (1982). *Black Children*. Baltimore: Johns Hopkins University Press.

Hansen, Donald A. (1986). Family-School Articulations: The Effects of Interaction Rule Mismatch. *American Educational Research Journal*, 23:643-659, Winter.

Henderson, A., Marberger, C. and Ooms, T. (1985). *Beyond the Bake Sale*. Columbia, MD: National Committee for Citizens in Education.

Henderson, A. (1981). *The Evidence Grows*. Columbia, MD: National Committee for Citizens in Education.

Henderson, A. (1987). *The Evidence Continues to Grow*. Columbia, MD: National Committee for Citizens in Education.

Hodgkinson, H. L. (1985). *All One System: Demographics of Education, Kindergarten Through Graduate School*. Washington: Institute for Educational Leadership.

Hoover-Dempsey, K. V., Bassler, O. C. and Brissie, J. S. (1987). Parent Involvement: Contributions of Teacher Efficacy, School SES, and Other School Characterisitics. *American Educational Research Journal*, 24:417-435, Fall.

Johnston, J. H. (1986). Dimensions of Family Participation in the Life of Schools. Paper presented to the annual convention of the National Association of Secondary School Principals, Orlando, Florida, March.

Johnston, J. H. (1989). Family Stories of School Achievement. Cincinnati: University of Cincinnati Center for Research on Literacy and Schooling.

Kamerman, S. B. and Hayes, C. D. (eds) (1983). *Children of Working Parents*. Washington: National Academy Press.

Lareau, Annette (1987). Social Class Differences in Family School Relationships. *Sociology of Education*, 60:73-85, April.

Lazar, I. and Darlington, R. B. (1978). Lasting Effects After Preschool. Ithaca, NY: Consortium for Longitudinal Studies. (ERIC: ED 175 523)

Leacock, E. B. (1969). *Teaching and Learning in City Schools*. New York: Basic Books.

Leitch, M. L. and Tangri, S.S. (1988). Barriers To Home-School Collaboration. *Educational Horizons*, Winter: 70-74.

Lewis, H. (1967). The Changing Negro Family. In *School Children in the Urban Slum*, J. Roberts (ed.). New York: The Free Press.

Lightfoot, S. L. (1978). *Worlds Apart: Relationships Between Families and Schools*. New York: Basic Books.

Lightfoot, S. L. and Carew, J. V. (1974). Individuation and Discrimination in the Classroom. Washington: Child Development Associates, Inc., Office of Child Development.

Linney, J. and Vernberg, E. (1983). Changing Patterns of Parental Employment and Family-School Relationships. In Hayes and Kamerman (eds), *Children of Working Parents*. Washington, DC: National Academy Press.

Lyons, P., et al. (1982). *Involving Parents*. Santa Monica, CA: System Development Corporation.

McDill, E. L., et al. (1969). *Educational Climates of High Schools: Their Effects and Sources*. Baltimore: Johns Hopkins University Center for the Study of Social Organization of Schools.

McPherson, G. (1972). *Small Town Teacher*. Cambridge, MA: Harvard University Press.

Medrich, E., et al. (1982). *The Serious Business of Growing Up*. Berkeley, CA: University of California Press.

Moles, O. (November, 1982). Synthesis of Research on Parent Participation in Children's Education. *Educational Leadership*, 40:3.

National Center for Educational Statistics (1984). Parent and Family Characteristics of 1982 High School Seniors. High School and Beyond Survey. Washington: The Center. Unpublished tabulation of data.

Ogbu, J. (1974). *The Next Generation*. New York: Academic Press.

Rich, Dorothy (1987). *Schools and Families: Issues and Actions*. Washington: National Education Association.

Slater, P. (1968). Social Change in the Democratic Family. In Bennis and Slater (ed), *The Temporary Society*. New York: Harper and Row.

Steinberg, L., et al. (1989). *Noninstructional Influences on High School Achievement: Contributions of Parents, Peers, Extracurricular Activities and Part time Work*. Madison: University of Wisconsin, Center on Effective Secondary Schools.

Swap, Susan McAllister (1987). *Enhancing Parent Involvement in Schools*. New York: Teachers College Press.

The Twenty-First Century Family (1990). *Newsweek* Special Issue, Winter-Spring.

Topping, K. J. (1986). *Parents as Educators*. Cambridge, MA: Brookline Books.

Walberg, H. J. (1984a). Families as Partners in Educational Productivity. *Phi Delta Kappan*, 65:397-400.

Walberg, H. J. (1984b). Improving the Productivity of America's Schools. *Educational Leadership*, 41:19-27.

Warren, R. (1973). The Classroom as Sanctuary for Teachers: Discontinuity and Social Control. *American Anthropologist*, 75:280-291.

Weiss, J. (1969). The Identification and Measurement of Environmental Process Variables Related to Self Esteem. Ph. D. Dissertation, University of Chicago.

Wilson, W. J. (1987). *The Truly Disadvantaged*. Chicago: University of Chicago Press.

Wolf, J. S. and Stephens, T. M. (1989). Parent/Teacher Conferences: Finding Common Ground. *Educational Leadership*, 47:2:28- 29.

Wolf, R. H. (1964). The Identification and Measurement of Environmental Process Variables Related to Intelligence. Ph. D. Dissertation, University of Chicago.

Zerchykov, R. (1984). *A Citizen's Notebook for Effective Schools*. Boston: Institute for Responsive Education.

PUBLICATIONS

National Middle School Association

The New American Family and the School
J. Howard Johnston (48 pages) $6.00

**Who They Are - How We Teach: Early Adolescents
and Their Teachers**
C. Kenneth McEwin and Julia T. Thomason (32 pages) $4.00

**The Japanese Junior High School: A View From The
Inside** Paul S. George (56 pages) $5.00

Schools in the Middle: Status and Progress
William M. Alexander and C. Kenneth McEwin (112 pages).......**$10.00**

**A Journey Through Time: A Chronology of Middle Level
Resources** Edward J. Lawton (36 pages) $5.00

**Dynamite in the Classroom: A How-To Handbook for
Teachers** Sandra L. Schurr (272 pages) $15.00

**Developing Effective Middle Schools Through Faculty
Participation. Second and Enlarged Edition**
Elliot Y. Merenbloom (108 pages)... $8.50

Preparing to Teach in Middle Level Schools
William M. Alexander and C. Kenneth McEwin (76 pages)............ $7.00

**Guidance in the Middle Level Schools: Everyone's
Responsibility** Claire Cole (34 pages)................................... $5.00

**Young Adolescent Development and School Practices:
Promoting Harmony** John Van Hoose & David Strahan
(68 pages).. $7.00

When the Kids Come First: Enhancing Self-Esteem
James A. Beane and Richard P. Lipka (96 pages)........................ $8.00

Interdisciplinary Teaching: Why and How
Gordon F. Vars (56 pages)... $6.00

Cognitive Matched Instruction in Action
Esther Fusco and Associates (36 pages)..................................... $5.00

The Middle School Donald H. Eichhorn (128 pages) $6.00

**Long-Term Teacher-Student Relationships: A Middle
School Case Study** Paul George (30 pages) $4.00

Positive Discipline: A Pocketful of Ideas
William Purkey and David Strahan (56 pages) $6.00

**Teachers as Inquirers: Strategies for Learning With and
About Early Adolescents** Chris Stevenson (52 pages) $6.00

Adviser-Advisee Programs: Why, What, and How
Michael James (75 pages) $7.00

What Research Says to the Middle Level Practitioner
J. Howard Johnston and Glenn C. Markle (112 pages) $8.00

Evidence for the Middle School
Paul George and Lynn Oldaker (52 pages) $6.00

Involving Parents in Middle Level Education
John W. Myers (52 pages) $6.00

Perspectives: Middle Level Education
John H. Lounsbury, Editor (190 pages) $10.00

The Theory Z School: Beyond Effectiveness
Paul S. George (106 pages) $6.00

**The Team Process: A Handbook for Teachers, Second and
Enlarged Edition** Elliot Y. Merenbloom (120 pages) $8.00

This We Believe NMSA Committee (24 pages) $3.50

Teacher to Teacher Nancy Doda (64 pages) $6.00

The Middle School in Profile: A Day in the Seventh Grade
John H. Lounsbury, Jean Marani, and Mary Compton (88 pages).... $7.00

**Early Adolescence: A Time of Change-Implications
for Schools** Videocassette (37 minutes) $75.00

**Early Adolescence: A Time of Change-Implications
for Parents** Videocassette and Utilization Guide (50 minutes)....$80.00

**NMSA, 4807 Evanswood Drive, Columbus, Ohio 43229-6292
(614) 848-8211   FAX (614) 848-4301**